The Spark

Ignite your passion

Arthur Kallos

Table of Contents

ignite your passion

For Leah, Markis, William & Sophia

You are the sparks in my life

ENDORSEMENTS

Great ideas alone are never enough to succeed in business or life. In this practical and helpful guide, Arthur Kallos explores the vital keys to turning your spark of inspiration into success that lasts.

Michael McQueen

Bestselling author, trend forecaster and business strategist

Inspiring! Arthur takes readers for an entertaining ride through his journey to small business realisation, which of course started with a Spark. His story is real and it's raw; Arthur's scope and honesty provokes thought around small business and the 'I CAN' attitude that is required to succeed. A must-read for anyone considering taking on the small business world. Prepare to be stimulated by a brilliant mind.

Theodore Dalkos

Senior Manager, Australian Taxation Office

I met Arthur when he was 'just a Teller' in a bank all those years ago and also as an accountant who has advised small business for more than 30 years. It was an absolute pleasure to read Arthur's book. It's such a refreshing and honest account of who should start their own business and most importantly why someone would go down that path. Everyone needs 'a spark' to take that first step out of stable employment, but most importantly there needs to be very real purpose to that spark and it must come direct from the heart Arthur outlines. Just making money will not keep the fire burning long into the future. Arthur's own story of helping his father in his take-away shop was inspirational, and my experience is that most of the truly successful business leaders I have worked with over the years also have a story inspired but some much bigger purpose. This book is a must-read not only for all involved in the financial services industry but also anyone contemplating starting their own business. And finally, I couldn't agree more with Arthur that everyone should experience the true magic of working in the 'job' that they alone created.

Nicholas Matsis CPA

Managing Director, NRM Johnson

The Spark is one man's story about the challenging nature of big business and the opportunities that abound in running your own small business; it will inspire you to back your own judgement.

Robert Reardon

Managing Director at Blackburn Insurance & Financial Services

Writing with the same passion, conviction and sincerity as his spoken word, Arthur successfully motivates and supports those around him—friends and business people alike—to want to achieve more.

Imants Didrichsons B.E. (Chem)

EDMS Business Analyst & myPlant Business Administrator (PE, OP, DSO)

I very much enjoyed reading Arthurs story. It's an inspirational and encouraging story with fantastic advice and a great insight into the future of business. Any business owner or person starting a new business can greatly benefit from reading this book.

Richard Fromberg

Australian Tennis Player

A great read with many learnings to take from the trials, challenges and victories experienced through Arthur's journey; the sparks that allowed him to learn, persist and grow as a person, a family man and a great leader. I highly recommend reading this book.

Sam Roshan

Director, eTraffic Group

Foreword

The Spark by Arthur Kallos highlights the riches that emerge when you follow the path that is right for you, rather than following a path of others.

An aspiring star in the financial services market, Arthur's career was suddenly halted in a corporate takeover. It's a situation that many can relate to; a career suddenly halted by a situation totally out of their control, where the impact on one's self-worth can spiral them into a dark valley where the actions you take next can dramatically determine your immediate future. What would you do?

Who would have thought that finding himself back in the family business, a small souvlaki shop, would be the shining light that led Arthur to grasp the changing landscape in the financial services industry? Whether it's the souvlaki shop or forming a financial services dealership, The Spark is what happens when your idea comes to life when you surround yourself with the right people and do it.

The Spark by Arthur Kallos is a journey that has commitment, passion, perseverance and inspiration, sometimes from the most unlikely sources. Above all The Spark has relevance. It is a book for business leaders who believe it's their time. The Spark is not a book about ideas that you read and then put on the shelf to collect dust, it's the ignition of the mind and soul.

Gordon Jenkins, The Visible Guy

*International keynote speaker and executive business coach supporting financial service leaders to future-proof their busine*ss.

"A boy comes to me with a spark of interest.

I feed the spark and it becomes a flame.

I feed the flame and it becomes a fire.

I feed the fire and it becomes a roaring blaze."

Cus D'amato, Mike Tyson's trainer

THE SPARK

What is the spark? The spark is an idea that is combined with an emotional experience. It creates a sudden rush. It creates hope. It stirs your heart and mind with thoughts of potential.

The spark is not just an idea. Ideas are a dime a dozen. It's more than that. It requires an emotional response, a stirring of your imagination and your spirit. When the spark happens, you know it, you feel it, and you have the time-sensitive opportunity to take ownership of that spark. The flip side is you can also let go of it, take no action, allow the emotion to detach from the idea, and let the spark fade away.

You have to keep the spark alive to see your idea become a reality in the world.

The spark is the starting point of an adventure. It's where initiative is first summoned. It's the trigger; the call to take action. To do that, to take action, you've got to climb across hurdles. You've got to push through challenges that can knock you out. You have to defy the odds and fight for victory. For the spark to move from idea to real-world activity, you also need to set yourself up so that you have the right support around you. Mentorship is an essential element of success. Most people who have tasted success attribute much of it to mentors who came into their lives at various times. While there are many people who can encourage you, guide you, and mentor you, ultimately it is up to you to feed the spark, to nurture it, and to take the kind of required continual action to turn it into a flame. As Mike Tyson's legendary trainer once said, when you feed the flame, it turns into a fire. When you feed the fire, it turns into a roaring blaze.

That's how you end up attempting and succeeding in things that truly matter to you. The spark is the call to try something you know has a purpose, great value, and would make your heart fully alive.

I believe you need to have the spark in life and career if you are going to do something meaningful and significant. I believe you need great mentors along the journey, you need a good system and community behind the scenes to support you, and you need belief in yourself to take the required action even when the evidence is not yet seen. You have to be willing to back yourself, and take risks, and do whatever it takes to get your idea, your spark, to catch on.

You can create a life by design. You can build a business that is deeply meaningful. You can live the dream.

It all starts with a spark.

"Small business isn't for the faint of heart.
It's for the brave, the patient, and the persistent.
It's for the overcomer."

Unknown

SMALL BUSINESS

Dad put down the phone. His hands were shaking.
"What's wrong?" I asked.

"It's your uncle. He's dying. If I don't get over there soon, I may not see him again."

"What are you going to do?"

He looked around at the shop, "Well, what can I do?"

"You gotta go," I said.

Again, he gazed around. "What about the shop?"

"I'll look after the shop," I replied without hesitation.

I had been out of work for a month, trying to figure out my next career move. For the first time in sixteen years, I wasn't working for a bank. I was at a crossroads in my life, a crisis point. When my dad told me about my uncle, I knew his problems were more important and urgent than mine. I didn't know what my next move should be regarding my career, but I knew my dad needed my help.

"What, you think you can do it?" he asked. Dad's little souvlaki shop was locally famous. Dad was a character and a great guy who took great pride in his work. He was a Greek immigrant who moved to Australia to create a better life for his family. It didn't come easily, but through sheer determination and a great work ethic, he built a great business. He had worked in that little souvlaki shop seven days a week, 14 hours a day, for 30 years.

"Well, yeah, sure I can do it. It's not rocket science." I said.

"Are you going to remember? You haven't worked in the shop since you were a kid."

It was strange to hear him say that. Standing there, hearing those words, I suddenly felt like I was coming full circle. I didn't leave the shop by choice sixteen years ago; I got kicked out by my dad because I didn't take personal ownership. I would just clock in and out; I thought I was better than being a kitchen hand in some little souvlaki shop. Dad sacked me because my attitude stank, and he was right to do it. So I left the family business, and that was what started my career with the bank. It turned out to be a career that I excelled in; in fact, it took me close to the top. However, that was over now, and I was back where I started.

Back in the shop.

Dad gave me a day's training, a quick refresher, and then I helped him get his passport renewed and tickets to Greece. Within one week he was overseas with his brother. He got to spend a week with him before he passed away. Mum and Dad stayed on for a few more months to mourn and spend time with the family who they hadn't been with for so long.

In the space of a month, I went from being one of the most senior managers in a bank in Australia to running dad's souvlaki shop. Talk about a change of career! But I didn't think of it like that. It was just the right thing to do. Dad needed me. He had always been there for me all those years. The shop had done amazing things for our family and paid for my education. I didn't get that back then, but I understood it this time around.

What I never really expected was how much I would get out of the experience, and how it was an opportunity for me. In fact, it was a catalyst in helping me learn on a sincere and honest level just what kind of career I wanted. It gave me the opportunity to try my hand in small business.

When you work in the bank, you don't need to worry about the things small business owners worry about constantly. For example, cash flow. In the bank, everything gets paid. You don't need to worry about it, you just have a sales budget, and you need to make it. In a small business, you've got a lot of variables. You have to get your own supplies, you've got to work with the rhythm of business. Along with the rhythm, you have to do the numbers; you have to get granular on the details. What comes in when, how much, what's your cost of sales? I had to break down the whole manufacturing process of a souvlaki. Sounds crazy, right? How much time does it take, and what are the costs, and what are the considerations actually to hand one over the counter?

I realised that nobody appreciates the amount of work that goes into that little souvlaki. It's not pressed meat or frozen meat that you re-sell. It's prepared from raw ingredients on the premises. There's a marinating process. There are days of marinating that occurs. There's stacking. There's the cooking and cutting all that kind of stuff; you have to break it right back. Regarding increasing profitability in the business, I had to work out how much lettuce was needed; I had to weigh everything. I needed the data. I had to break it right down to see the numbers. Dad had trained his eye to understand the ratios and portions over the years. I had to learn that level of precision immediately.

That was an excellent exercise because all I'd ever done in the past was breaking down numbers in the sense of the product sales through bank channels. Now I was breaking down numbers to sell a souvlaki. It was small scale, but it's what small business is all about. The experience helped me realise what it feels and looks like to be right in the thick of running a business. What I'm most thankful for, however, isn't just the business lessons it taught me; it was the re-ignition of my passion for business. It gave me back the desire to do something that was meaningful.

Working in dad's business gave me my spark back.

"Decision is the spark that ignites action. Until a decision is made, nothing happens."

William A Peterson

DECISIONS

"I've never this felt sore before." That was the thought running through my mind. It had been another long day running my dad's shop. Day twenty. I had been working seven days a week just as my dad had done all his life, and I was beyond exhausted. I had just finished closing the shop on a big Saturday night. I had done the big clean, a big mop, and a big wipe down. I finished all the cleaning and got in my car, heading for home. It was 3:30 AM.

My body was in agony, and I'm a fit person. I'm in the gym every day, but regardless I had never felt that kind of soreness before.

I could hardly steer, my hands were aching that much. I sat at that red light, and I said, "Oh god, I can't believe how much pain I'm in." Then, suddenly, I thought about my dad, and how he had been doing this for 30 years, but how? How did he keep it up? How did he handle it for so long? I just couldn't fathom how he'd been able to do it seven days a week, 100 hours a week, for that long.

The lights turned green, but I didn't move. I stayed right where I was, and this feeling of guilt came over me. I started crying. Once the tears started, I couldn't stop them. They poured out of me. I don't know whether it was a combination of the emotional rollercoaster I'd been through over those initial three weeks of running the shop and the transition. Maybe I was releasing a lot of anguish about how things were turning out, all the uncertainty about my career and future. I think it was also a release of the guilt I felt about my dad, and how much he had done for our family and me, and I had never even noticed; I had never honoured him for it.

I hit the steering wheel in frustration and scolded myself, "Where the hell have you been? Where were you? You didn't once go see your father to say, 'Hi, how's it going dad?'"

I reflected with shame how throughout my 20's before I left for Sydney, I hardly ever went and saw my dad. I slowly started driving home. When the tears had run their course, I remember saying to myself, "Well, I'm in it now, I'm in it for dad and myself and my family, and I've just gotta keep on pushing through. It's hard, but this is how it is."

That moment set my priorities right. I realised that at the end of the day, the only ones that you answer to are your family. Whether you have a wife, kids, husband, step-kids, whatever combination, or you may not be married; you owe it to your family; you owe it to yourself. That's all that matters. That's the only people that ultimately care for you. There's a lot of people that you meet in life, in your career, and in that frame or in that moment in time, yeah, it's a partnership, and they'll care for you. The ones that will be there for you, through thick and thin, are your family.

These days I run my own Advisory Financial Dealer Group that supports and empowers independent financial planners. When I speak with financial planners thinking of working within my Group, one of the things I always say to them is that by starting your own business, you can build something for your family. I think it's the greatest motivation, to do it for them rather than anyone else. I think everyone should work for themselves. Looking back now, I think everyone should have the job that they've created rather than applied for, and start work for themselves. I think it's going to be like that more and more purely by the way the market is going, but people still need to make a choice and take the leap of faith. I do see the market shifting dramatically to a freelancing model. I also see the big institutions removing their face to face sales force because I think they've worked out that they can't afford it anymore if they want to keep their profits where they are, or divest themselves from the Financial Planning model altogether. They know they have to change their sales models, and that will affect how they hire and fire their workforce also; but regardless, I think everybody should work for themselves.

Throughout my whole career, I was always in a system. In my case, the banking system. The first part of my career I was a great fit, the system seemed to mould around me. I was given senior leadership positions, put on leadership courses, handed opportunities to advance. I was being groomed to be a GM in a bank, one of the biggest in Australia. I was a hot shot and had a big chip on my shoulder. It didn't matter because the system loved me, it seemed to work for me, elevating me and giving me opportunity. I won major awards throughout my 20's. My star was rising. I did whatever it took to rise in the ranks, including living in Sydney during the week and flying home to my wife and child on weekends. I was relentless, and I was being rewarded by the system for my efforts and loyalty.

But then our bank got bought by an even bigger bank, and instead of being the golden boy in the system, I was on the wrong side of a war between two companies trying to merge into one. In the end, all my supporters and sponsors in management from my bank were removed, left or were re-deployed. I held on because I was determined to keep my position as a rising star in the banking world. I kept my job, but things changed, and they never went back to the way they were before.

The first half of my career in the banking world I shot almost to the top without much friction, but towards the back end of my banking career I was compromising myself and my integrity trying to fit back in, but the system had changed, and I no longer fit. No matter what I tried, it was bending and breaking me. The environment changed, and I changed to still fit, but it cost me my authenticity. I was fighting for survival. I hated the new environment but wasn't brave or wise enough to walk away. Some called me resilient; maybe I was just being stubborn. Regardless, one thing was true: I was losing myself, and I didn't even know it.

There were many incidents where I felt the spark in my various roles in the bank. When I was the decision maker, it was great; but so often nobody is the ultimate decision maker. It's crazy but true. Often it is left to a group of leaders, and none of them are willing to put their necks on the line and make a decision that is outside their comfort zone, so the decision is no decision.

When you are an ideas person and optimistic, you want to make a difference. That is what drove me and I was always looking for opportunities to do something innovative and important. I remember when the government announced a change in the regulations around banking that caused the spark to light up in me. It was an exciting moment because I saw how our bank could create a fantastic offer in response to the new regulations.

I felt that the initiative was very noble, and it fit with the bank's 'stated' purpose. If we got the green light to build and scale it, it would help increase access to advice by helping people in remote areas get access to advice by streaming our advisers into the branches. It was aimed at helping people in country towns in regional Australia, where people couldn't get access to an advisor. I thought, "Why don't we video conference them into the branch and they can have a face to face conversation with an advisor?"

Although it was very viable and purpose-driven, it just didn't appeal to any of the senior management to invest in that idea. It wasn't just a good idea; it was good business. Still, it didn't matter. But I couldn't let it go. I pushed when I was expected to give up. I looked for other ways to make it happen when the first and most apparent way turned out to be a dead end. I still didn't truly get it that if the decision makers didn't like it, it didn't matter how good an idea it was, it would be torpedoed. It had no chance. At the time, I just didn't want to believe that, so I sat down and did the numbers and thought, "I'm leading a team right now that has a lot of under-utilisation." I had people in my team, whose role at the time was to give over the phone based advice via inbound calls. I knew there was capacity for new projects because the phones weren't ringing non-stop. My idea was to get these planners in front of clients through video conferencing in remote branches. We could make money out of this because one planner could service multiple branches around the country inside of one day. The numbers made sense in that way. I thought, "I'm paying the salary expense anyway. I'm paying for a full-time equivalent salary, but I want to get a better utilisation of my staff and create more value for our customers." In my mind, any increase in revenue we generated was going to be all upside. It was a better utilisation of my team's time and resources and my team wanted to do it!

The catch was I needed to set up the infrastructure. I needed to get the screens in the branches and all that kind of stuff. I wasn't getting the full support of the General Manager of Advice who was very cautious by nature. But the spark was there and I wanted it to happen, so I tried another path. I recategorised what I was planning as an IT initiative. I approached the general manager of IT, and he funded me. We started the project with about half a million dollars. We bought all the equipment and identified which branches would best utilise this service and partner up. So, we operationalised it; we deployed the IT and handled the IT setup in the branch. Then customers would come in and book financial planning appointments in the branch, in front of that TV screen, with one of our advisors in Sydney. We enabled and trained the financial planners to advise via the online delivery method, then integrated visual tools, graphs and diagrams. What a great client experience!

It was an innovative pilot. It had never been done before and it garnered national media attention in The Australian newspaper. We were featured in the paper as an Australian first.

For a time it looked like the spark was catching on. The IT team caught the spark and got passionate about the project, saying, "We can do this so much better, we can help people using technology." The whole push was around technology, how can technology help people do better? Rather than handling the advice through the traditional channels, we were enterprising, thinking that we can use IT platforms to deliver advice. The irony was, in the end, the GM of Advice, who was fearful of such change was forced to respond to the reporter who wrote the article. He played the political card, I guess, and said, "We want many of these running in the country shortly." There was no real intent to do it.

Even though I had the spark, and the spark caught on to the whole IT department, the initiative wasn't funded for expansion, and after a few months was shelved entirely.

This was just one of a long list of situations where the spark happened within me, or within one of my colleagues, only to be extinguished for no good reason. The problem with that happening, is you start hardening yourself up, you start being more cynical, and you start ignoring those spark moments and just play the game the way the decision makers want you to play: Safe and aligned to the status quo. The lesson I learned through the process is that no matter how good your idea is, no matter how well it can help people, no matter how much sense it can make, if you don't have the ultimate decision-maker on your side you'll never execute your idea in a meaningful and sustainable way. The reason is simple: because you're challenging the status quo. You may see it as significant innovation, but all too often it is understood by those higher up as unnecessary change and disruption. Rather than being rewarded due to your passion for the business and the customer, you're seen as not falling in line within the organisation. You're not seen as bringing solutions, but creating problems. What a shame! We could have helped so many people. Think about these people in regional country towns, who fly to a hospital to get medical advice, or they get medical advice through video. They were using video to get medical advice, so why couldn't you use video to get financial advice?

You can have a spark and you can run the numbers and you can feel very confident about it, and you can see that there's purpose behind it, but the chances of it being embraced and implemented are close to zero unless you happen to get the decision maker on side. The bigger the organisation, the harder that task is. I realise it's not the problem of any individual. The giant system itself works against the spark. It protects itself from risk and favours the status quo. Those who play by those rules prosper in the system, those that don't get worn down and eventually discarded.

The challenge—I slowly came to realise—lay not in fighting the system, it's too big and too set in its ways; no, the real challenge is answering the question: Are you brave enough to step outside the corporate setting and become your own decision maker?

"No legacy is so rich as honesty."

William Shakespeare

HONESTY

"You were meant to be great, you were becoming great, but something happened to you."

Those were the words of my peer, a fellow leader in the bank. She wasn't trying to be mean. She was blunt, but not intentionally cruel. There was a meaning behind it that I think she knew would serve me well once I figured it out.

It was my last day in the office. I had resigned. At the time I blew off the comment. I had other things to worry about.

For years I had been travelling back and forwards, from Adelaide to Sydney, every week. I became frustrated and over time began to feel like an outsider even though I was still inside. I knew the end was coming when I had asked for the opportunity to work flexibly, some days in Adelaide and some days in Sydney, but it wasn't accepted. My boss knew as well as I did what that meant. I would have to leave the organisation. My second son was due to be born, and I had to be with my family. I had put my wife Leah and son Markis in second place to my career for too long. It was unfair and unsustainable, and I had made the firm decision months ago to put my family first, come what may; being away from them so much wasn't negotiable anymore. That meant I had to resign from my position in Sydney and look for a new role in Adelaide. I had put my feelers out in the Adelaide banking scene, but it wasn't a simple transition. Because I had risen so high in Sydney's corporate world and had so much success in my various senior roles, everyone I talked with said I was overqualified. There were plenty of jobs and opportunities in Sydney, but they were no longer an option. It would ruin my family. I had to put my roots down in my hometown of Adelaide again and trust a job would surface when I did.

I was frustrated with how things played out. I had given my life to the bank. I had poured my heart and soul into my work. I couldn't have given more, but it didn't matter because as soon as I left that office for the last time, I'd be forgotten. That's how it worked. My peer made that remark, and at the time it bounced off me, but it didn't leave me. The words replayed in my mind over the following months. I knew what she meant, and I knew what happened—the real reason—but I didn't want to admit it.

The truth I didn't want to face was that I hated myself.

That resentment towards myself had come through and altered the direction of my career. I didn't start off hating myself. At first, I hated the situation. Slowly, I lost my spark, my passion, my desire to make meaningful change, and in turn I didn't like who I was becoming. I hated the situation and got more and more frustrated. I was conflicted. I wanted to do things that I wasn't allowed to do. I was fighting a system but I couldn't win that fight. Instead, I just got more and more frustrated and started tarnishing my reputation. During that time I was still searching for that brilliance, that spark, to empower me to overcome it all. Despite myself, I stayed longer than I should have and tried to change things, to overcome all the odds, to make a difference. I couldn't let my ego accept defeat. I kept acting like I could overcome it. In the end, I lost to the system. It put out my spark, and it beat me. It caused me to change how I felt about myself and my integrity.

Through that experience, I learned that no matter how good you are, and no matter how much ability you have, if you don't have the right network into the right spots in the organisation, you can't change anything; it's a futile exercise. It's utterly futile, and then you go through those negative emotions of resentment, at least for me, it turned me against myself. I got to the point I didn't like myself. How tragic! These days I'm happier than I've ever been, but if I hadn't changed direction, who knows where I would have ended up emotionally.

"Something happened to you." Even in the moment, I knew what she was talking about; I didn't want to admit it then. I didn't want to have to face it, but something did happen to me. I did change. I lost my spark, my positiveness,

my energy. I lost it, and I became negative and not very pleasant to be around. I was moody and at times unprofessional. In the end, I was only harming myself, but I was not mature enough to realise the situation and make the decision to pull myself out of it. I removed myself because of the timing of my second son being born. That, thankfully, forced me to make a decision. If he wasn't coming along, I still would have been battling that same battle because I'm resilient and relentless to get something through. I would have been living the classic example of someone who cuts off their nose to spite their face. I would have just stayed in that situation just to prove a point, to prove I was resilient and right, but to who? That's the irony of it all. Nobody even gave a shit! They couldn't have cared less about my point. Even if I did get my point across, they wouldn't have cared.

I think a lot of people are trapped in a situation where they're trying to change a situation when they are better off cutting their losses and going out and creating their own thing.

In the corporate system, most people just don't care. You think you're proving a point, but nobody cares. They're not going to wake up the next morning and go, "Oh yeah, he was right."

Forgetaboutit!

We're so consumed in our own selves. We think that others will be as equally invested. We're just fooling ourselves. In that situation, you're better off to simply stop lying to yourself and focus your energy on following your dreams and making the decisions to enable them to come to life. Put your energy into that, rather than energy into a negative stream.

"We have to dare to be ourselves, however frightening or strange that self may prove to be."

May Sarton

AUTHENTICITY

"**A**rthur? Is that you?"

I was busting my ass churning out souvlakis for all the drunks coming out of the clubs, as usual. I looked up to see who was talking to me. My heart sank. It was a banker with whom I had had some dealings in the past. He looked at me with half confusion and half disgust.

"What the hell are you doing working here? Aren't you meant to be some hot shot in Sydney?"

I wanted the ground to swallow me up. I wanted to disappear. At that moment, I felt my whole body sink. His words had the force of a sledgehammer. I had never felt that before. It was the moment when what I was doing hit home. I was a hot shot banker, and I was now working in a takeaway joint. This wasn't a game; the situation was my real life.

"Oh God, what have I done?" I thought. "I'm here. I'm not in the bank. I'm not a respected leader. I'm here in my dad's souvlaki shop and I don't know what's next. I've worked all my life to build this big banker profile, and in this world—the real world—it means nothing."

I realised that everything I had been and done, just ceased to matter, because behind that counter I was seen as a lesser person by everyone. It wasn't just my former peer who saw me that way, so did the drunk uni student who threw his souvlaki at me for a laugh. So did everyone who didn't bother saying thank you when I served them. I was coming into that job full of heart, willing to give every customer a great experience just as my dad had done for 30 years, and I experienced how little appreciation people had. In the bank, I was looked up to, respected and acknowledged. When that banker said those words, "What happened to you?" it hurt, because, to a large degree, I didn't know the answer.

I remember thinking to myself that I had a choice. I could reply to him graciously, or I could tell him where to go and tell him what I really thought. I took it as an opportunity to learn a lesson, to overcome my natural instinct at that moment, which was to attack, and instead learn to be gracious. When you're in that corporate environment, and in the middle of a corporate merger of epic proportion, you're fighting every day, and your natural inclination becomes to attack or to bite back. Offence was the best defence. I had to change that because I don't think that approach helped me through the latter journey of my career in the bank, and it came from a defensive stance, where you're trying to defend yourself. You essentially attack.

So I swallowed my pride and thought to myself, "Here's an opportunity to respond correctly."

I took a big breath and said, "I'm just here helping my dad." And I rolled his souvlaki and served it with a forced smile. That was enough. I didn't have to say anything more. I didn't have to explain anything. I didn't have to justify myself. I was there because I was helping my dad, and that was fine, because my dad helped me all those years ago when I was just a kid who thought he was better than working in a souvlaki shop.

I remember that moment because I was able to use it to grow personally. I had the humility to swallow my pride, and hold onto that moment, and use it as a motivator. For me, that was a big lesson, because I knew one day that experience would serve me well. I accepted it as part of the journey, and so that was a bit of a rock-bottom moment, where reality kicked in. I had fought so long to be seen in a certain way in the corporate system, and suddenly I was seen as a failure in a souvlaki shop. It was a pretty big hit, but it was the start of an exceptional journey.

What I learned was that to leave corporate and start your own thing, you have to be willing to be more honest and real, and grow personally, because the rules in small business are a lot different to those in corporate. To be ready to run your own business you need to know yourself because if you don't know yourself, you won't know how to communicate yourself. If you don't know how to communicate yourself, people won't understand you and people won't trust you. All the moments in my dad's shop challenged me at the time, but what they did was put me back in touch with my emotions, with what is real and with what matters most in life.

If you don't know who you are and what you're about, you've got gaps in your armour or your toolkit. Those gaps can be hidden in the corporate world, but in the real world, people will see through them. I had a lot of holes in my development. Through my career in the bank, I wasn't forced to attend to certain aspects of my personal development. Yes, I received a lot of training and development in the bank, but there's nothing like, "Hey, you've got no income, and you've got no job. What are you going to do about it?" That's the ultimate personal development.

The reality is that I had a lot of gaps, and I had to go through that experience running dad's shop to learn about myself, and what I found is that those lessons built out my character. The experience created a lot of character, and it's amazing that anytime I share these stories with people, it gets me to my goal. I've realised that people want to know about people. We live the majority of our working careers in a mask, where we put up a front because we're scared to show who we really are. If you do that over an extended enough period, you lose track of who you are. You lose touch with yourself, and the mask becomes something, makes you something you're not. Then there's always friction because people know on a subconscious level that they're dealing with a mask but they still deal with you because you work for the bank and there is a greater level of trust there. The corporate brand overshadows your brand, restricting your ability to shine.

When you're pushing the brand of another entity, like a bank, you're not presenting yourself. You have to buy into that corporate entity. There might be aspects of it that you don't agree with, but you do it anyway because it puts food on your table. The longer you do it, the more you risk losing yourself.

The further down that track you go the harder it is to turn back. The road ended abruptly for me and forced me to change direction. It was traumatic, but it was a cleaner break that ultimately paved the way for me to recreate myself.

The way I went full circle is ironic in the sense that I had to recreate myself back where I started. I was nobody when I was 16 in the shop helping out with the fridges, and doing the kitchen hand work, and all that kind of stuff. I was back to having no identity again at the age of 35. I had to start again, and find out who I really was and what it was I was all about. The timing was uncanny because at the same time the marketplace had also changed where consumers now really want to know more about people, like who they are, and who they're dealing with.

These days, anytime I share my story people want to hear about it. It doesn't matter if it's a business setting or not; everyone wants the real deal, they want to hear authentic stories and get to know the real person. In this new marketplace, you're not doing yourself any favours by hiding yourself or playing the corporate mask wearing game. You have to get real.

My advice is that when you're starting your own business, you have to be 100% authentic and transparent. Otherwise, don't do it, because for starters you'll be fooling people if they do business with you if you're not genuine, open, and honest about yourself. Secondly, if you are authentic, you'll also be successful, because that is what the marketplace is looking for. People want to have a genuine connection with other people. Some people have a greater range of frequency, some people have a greater range of attraction, but we all attract certain people. If you send out that message clearly and concisely, you'll attract your fair share of customers in line with your ability and capacity.

Anyone with a base level of ability that can communicate themselves clearly, transparently, and authentically will attract people that will want to do business with you. It's just human nature, but as soon as you put anything in the way of that, you break that frequency. You cut that message off. I know that over time what happened is every time that I shared a bit more of myself, it was well received, and it gives me more confidence to reveal a little bit more about myself. Now I'm at the point where I have no issue in talking about my journey.

Recently, I stood up in front of 100 financial planners at a professional development day and I told them about selling souvlakis in a professional forum. I related my experience transforming Dad's business back to financial planning practice transformation. It was just my story, but it resonated deeply. I didn't want to go out there and just talk numbers because numbers don't connect like authentic stories do.

People connected with my story, and they will with yours too when you get comfortable sharing it. I had all these planners coming up to me after the presentation saying, "Yeah, that was a really interesting story. I was captivated by it." They know that event organisers don't put anyone in front of 100 planners to talk about their business, so the audience knew I had the business expertise behind me. I got an overwhelming response from people who related to my story and felt energised to make changes in their business. I passed on my spark.

At that point, I was freely sharing my story anyway, because I understood how powerful doing it was and how the process works. You have to start where you are. You have to start sharing to the level you are comfortable. Over time what happens is the more you give, the more you get back. You get to the point where you are freely sharing and are proud of who you are, and provided you have a good moral compass, and a good value system, why shouldn't you be proud of who you are? Just build the confidence and the courage to show who you are, but I understand it does take time because everyone's got a different background. Everyone's got a different set of experiences.

To get to where you want to go, and to achieve what you want to achieve in business, I think people see through those that don't show who they are, who don't reveal themselves. It's the people that reveal themselves honestly, graciously, and with humility, who do well in business.

"I'm always looking for
the creative spark. Always."
Jimmy Page

OPPORTUNITY

When I quit the bank and returned to Adelaide to start afresh, there was a real shift beginning to take place in the marketplace. At the time, I'm not sure if many noticed it, but it was the start of the shift away from traditional big brands holding all the power to personal brands delivered through social media platforms. I didn't quite understand at the time, but I knew something was looming in the sense that a personal brand could be effective without a massive marketing budget or a marketing brand presence to deliver your personal value proposition.

When you're working for a large organisation, you're spending your whole time delivering the proposition of the organisation. People will always deal with you because they trust you, but that's only half of it. The other half of their buying decision is based on the fact that they feel the brand itself is big and well known. They know the history of a large organisation. That's changed now. Today, consumers are much more interested in the personal brand rather than the corporate one because employees come and go. Consumers today are more than happy to get to know an individual, see them on social media and connect with them. It holds the lion's share of decision making today.

Coming out of corporate at the time, it was fresh in my mind. I started thinking about personal branding at a strategic level and learning how to leverage it as a small business owner because I began to believe that was the way the market would move. Five years later and it's now started to become a real reality. People are sceptical of corporate brands, but they are listening to and buying from personal brands in droves. It's perhaps the biggest shift in how people decide on purchasing the market has ever seen.

I was pondering on just this idea as I leaned on the counter, waiting for the next customer, and I realised a great strength about the shop was dad had a brand. He'd done all the hard yards and had already put in a massive amount of effort and time over the years. People knew him. He was an authentic guy. He had personality. He always made an effort to make genuine connections with his customers and his community. He had developed a personal brand but it was all offline. He didn't understand how he had built it and had no idea how to leverage it. The problem was technology caught up, and just having an offline brand like my dad's was no longer enough. I made a list of a variety of ways to grow your personal brand that dad wasn't capitalising on.

When Mum and Dad left for Greece, I was given control of the business. I started thinking about dad's brand, and how we could leverage it better, to create more opportunity in the marketplace. I started to look at the website, the social media platforms, and thought, "We can use these channels to reconnect with previous customers and let everybody know that we're still here, create excitement and invite them to come in again to see what was going on!"

I got to work on getting a new website up, and we got the Facebook page up and running. That immediately started getting traction because Dad was such a notorious character in the community, in a good way. He had built such a strong personal brand offline, that online people immediately latched onto it.

The other thing that was becoming popular at the time were food vans. I saw it was a bit of a craze, and I thought to myself, "Why wouldn't we be able to have a successful food van business?" One that did sports events, catering, festivals, and all that kind of stuff, because Dad's product is well known.

I remember thinking about the food van concept and questioning myself, thinking, "Oh, should I do this expansion?" At the time I was sitting with my mate Theo, and he said to me, "Mate, you can't fail. You can't fail, you won't fail."

And I replied, "Oh yeah, what about this, and what about that?" I was trying to talk myself out of it. He looked at me and just smiled, saying, "Mate, just do it, it won't fail. You've thought it out, it's perfect, you won't fail," and he was right. Now, at the end of the day, it wasn't his money on the line, so he was probably a little bit more liberal with his feedback. I was the one, at the end of the day, investing in the build of the van and the business. But he was still honest, and he was a positive guy, he was a great, optimistic, go-getter himself. You need these kind of people around you. The kind of people who will feed your belief rather than your doubt. It's monumentally helpful to have people around you who will give you their honest opinion, but if they think that you can make it, they'll do all they can to feed that belief, they'll encourage you that you're onto something good, or you've done well. Theo was that kind of friend. He'd be the first person to pick up the phone and say, "Well done, mate, you did an excellent job, congratulations. You deserve all the reward." You need people around you like that. People who are very complimentary, but they'll also have the hard conversations with you too. Surround yourself with the right people that give you the honesty that you need to make sure that you don't make mistakes, but at the same time help you to back yourself.

So I started building the food van immediately, and it was an instant hit when we took it to market.

Within three months our food van was getting into all the festivals, and getting priority bookings because of dad's reputation and brand. Event organisers wanted us at their events because it made them look good. We tapped into a market more than willing to do business with us, but it required a different approach to win that kind of work. We had to take what was great about the shop and put it on wheels. It was entrepreneurial. We were getting invited to all these different festivals. We also did a lot of party catering. People trusted the brand, and they were happy for us to come into their home, and deliver our catering services to first birthdays, christenings, all that kind of stuff.

Finally, we realised that the people that used to come into the shop years and years ago were turning 40 and 50, so we're getting all the 40th's, we're getting all the 50th's, we're getting all these birthday events, 100 – 200 people at a time. That's how the food van business was born, and it's still alive today, still going strong five years down the track. It was one of these ideas that I had, that just came to me leaning against the counter, looking out into the street. Thinking to myself going, "There's gotta be a better way. There's gotta be a better way."

The reason I was able to develop that food van business, I believe, was because nothing stood in my way. There were no bureaucratic roadblocks or committee meetings. I had the opportunity to take action. There was no, "Well, I want to do this, and I can't do this because of that." Nothing was stopping me, but myself, and I didn't want to hit the brakes, I wanted to hit the accelerator. That's what is so great about being in control of your own business. It's your creation; you build it through your creativity and imagination, and nobody is stopping you. When I realised that, I felt the spark. The whole idea came to me within a few seconds, I saw it almost in slow motion, and thought, "Oh my God, this could work." The spark energised me and I said, "Right, this is what I'm gonna do." That was the goal, to get things moving. Dad was going to be away for a few months, and I saw that as my window of opportunity because if he got back he would put a stop to everything. I had a time limit. I had to get it done. Within three months we tripled the revenue of the business.

When my dad got back, his first instinct was to chastise me.

"What is all this? Who paid for all this? Arthur, what have you done?" The shop had been transformed. The business looked great, but to dad he just saw change, and he was slow to change; he also equated change with expenses. The last thing he wanted to do was come home to debt.

"You better have a damn good explanation!"

I could see in his eyes that he was preparing himself to kick me out of his shop for the second time in his life.

"I do Dad, here."

I handed him the bank balance for the business.

He looked at the numbers, then up at me, then back down to the paper. Finally, he looked up again, and said, "What are you doing, selling drugs?"

"No Dad, I'm selling your personal brand—and the marketplace is loving it."

That was a great moment for me, and it was a revelation for my dad. He was now smiling like a kid caught with his hand in the cookie jar. "What is this personal brand? What does that mean?"

Dad didn't get it, but it was alright because I was there to build and leverage it for him. He didn't even value his personal brand. The 30 years of serving the drunk and disorderly had taken its toll, but his resiliency is that of legendary status and he hung in long enough which then allowed me to scale his business and dramatically improve the result in such a short time frame.

What about you? Do you value your personal brand?

How much value to you put on your personal brand? How much do you invest in it? We all have a brand. If you are in business, you need to take responsibility over yours, and if you want to go into business for yourself, you need to understand that when you build a strong personal brand, you can not only compete with the corporate giants, you can topple them over and win business before they do. The days of big brands getting the work just because they are big are over. The entire marketplace is evolving and shifting, and it is to the advantage of the small business owners. There's never been such an opportunity to start and successfully grow a business as right now. The risk is starting to lie in the big institutions and their endless restructuring, redundancies, and replacing humans with robots. If you are thinking of leaping at some point in the future out of corporate and into your own practice, start working on your personal brand now. The big corporates are gearing their machine to seek services from the growing freelance economy. There will be less employed sellers and as a result less middle management to oversee these sellers.

Get prepared. Become known for your authenticity, your willingness to share knowledge and add value. The opportunity is there for the taking, and the person standing in the way of building a great personal brand today isn't your boss or the corporation you work for—you guessed it, it's you. The good news is with a bit of bravery, decision making, and action you're the easiest obstacle to get out of the way.

"You have to find what sparks a light
in you so that you, in your own way,
can illuminate the world."
Oprah Winfrey

ACTION

What I learned through my experience building and expanding my dad's business was that when you are the owner of a small business, you've got freedom—the obstacles you face in corporate don't exist. The only obstacle is your fears, and if you can overcome them, you can overcome anything. With your own business, you've got nothing getting in your way. You've got emotional skin in the game, you've got the imagination, you've got the creative ability. Then, you just need to execute with your practical experience that you've earned over the years in your career.

If you are a financial planner, for example, you've got the practical experience. You've likely gone through the bank for many years. You know what to do, but you need to back yourself and your imagination. You need the desire to create. If you want to go into business for yourself, you need the spark, and you need the right people around you to feed the spark to turn it into a flame.

Looking back at the end of three months working in my dad's business and bringing about such a turnaround, I became aware of just how much impact you can have when you have the freedom to go for it. If you're in small business, you can make significant changes, take bigger risks, and get bigger rewards. It's easier to fine tune little bits and pieces. One degree change in direction over five years dramatically changes the direction of the business over that period, because that one degree becomes more and more and more of a lever.

The big lesson I learned there was about impact. You can have an idea and take action on it and create a significant level of impact in a short time—and you get 100% of the reward. That's when I decided I was never going back to corporate. I said to myself, "This is where I want to be, small business."

When you run your own business, you can create change, immediate impact, and get the benefit of it. That's what I learned. I also learned if you want to succeed in small business, you have to back yourself and all the pieces have to come together, but there's always a leap of faith. The opportunity to take action is available right now. It's never been better to follow your spark and take hold of the opportunity because the market is changing in favour of small business owners—but will you capitalise on it? That's a question you need to answer.

The shift in the marketplace—across all service-based industries—is a game changer for small business. It is a huge opportunity for those smart enough to take advantage of the changing rules of business. The market is going towards a merit-based, self-regulated local market model on the back of the social media infrastructure. It is creating a phenomenal opportunity for small business owners to build their profile in their local market and win business that big business can't. It's up to you to make yourself known in your local market. It means you need to align yourself with systems that will give you rewards based on merit, such as review sites, because that's an excellent way to be seen. That's good for your personal brand and it makes you treat every customer as your first.

I remember when I got trained at the bank, that's what they said to me, treat every customer—as mundane as the job is,withdrawal slip, after withdrawal slip—as if it's your first customer. I still remember my first customer experience. It was a $400 withdrawal request, and I was shitting myself. I had to count the money five times to make sure I was getting it right, with a smile.

Alternatively, a merit-based market is disastrous in a big corporate because one bad seed in their organisation can tarnish their brand for everyone. Employee attitudes have changed, their affinity for the brand has diminished as they hop from job to job and brand to brand. The career banker is extinct. A job in a bank is a stepping stone to another job elsewhere.

They are losing the inside out control of their brand, and the more integrated review sites and social feedback loops come into the consumer buying process, the more difficult this will become for big business. But for you and me, for those who are playing all out in their own business, who control their own quality of work, it's the opportunity of a lifetime. There's never been a better time for someone to go out on their own and build their own business. It's a window of opportunity, and it's there for the talking if you take it seriously. This new kind of system, one that is merit-based and publicly transparent, that encourages self-regulation, means the cost of compliance will be decreased rather than increased. When businesses self-regulate, you can reduce the costs of compliance, because of the assistance the force of self-regulation brings. The market needs this as ultimately it is consumers who feel the effect of these costs being passed on in the form of higher prices and potentially opt out of receiving advice. That's a lose-lose situation.

If you are known locally for the quality of your work, people will find you; your personal brand will have huge exposure online and through word of mouth. The marketplace has fundamentally changed. In today's social media and internet transparent world, you don't need to be part of a big corporate brand. You need to take ownership of your own. You can be known as a person in your local market that is honest, hardworking and does a bloody good job. That's how you get business. You don't need to be part of a big brand where you sit in this branch, and the branch is trying to force customers into you.

It's the pull versus push strategy. The corporate push strategy is a costly one. Think how hard these employees get driven because they've got to meet the quotas; they've got to hit their numbers to justify the expense of their salary. Whereas the pull, or the gravity model, being in a local market, allows people to gravitate to you if you understand these three elements of the new marketplace: Local market strategies, self-regulating, merit-based systems, and social media platforms. The gravity model can only be run when a business is local and agile; it's a good model. It's cheaper to operate which means you don't have to charge an arm and a leg for your advice. You can advise a fair rate which will win you more business The big corporates can't take this approach even if they wanted to because they aren't agile or allow employees to promote themselves freely on social media. They are the opposite, and right there is your advantage if you leap into strategically running your own business.

People are engaging with other people online for business reasons at an accelerated rate, and that's just going to happen more and more. People can resist, but it will continue to build momentum until it merely becomes the standard way business gets done. I remember food delivery of groceries, started in 1990. There was a company in South Australia that would deliver your groceries and your fruit to the door. Everyone said, "That's a stupid idea." It wasn't stupid; it was brilliant, they were just before their time. Now, you've got Lite 'n Easy and all these other companies doing it. Even Woolworths does it. It's not so dumb anymore. In fact, it was never dumb; it's just that the market wasn't ready for it, and the technology hadn't been developed yet. The technology for that original company was the fax! You faxed your order in. That was the technology. Now you just go online, click-click-click, and you've got this infrastructure and procurement that delivers that thing fresh to your door every day.

The market's ready for it now. The market wasn't prepared, and the infrastructure wasn't created, back in 1990. Technology's changing all that. Technology has outgrown the pace of business innovation concepts. Previously, business was always trying to innovate, but the technology wasn't there, and it slowed everything down. Now, technology is miles ahead. It will never be slower than innovative ideas again. It's creating a major shift because what's happening is the people delivering innovative solutions aren't going to provide it to the mainstream in the way they want anymore. The mainstream has always been resistant to new ways of doing things, but now they are going to have to accept it because there won't be any other option. Big business will change dramatically, and the mainstream isn't going to like it, but they won't have any choice but accept the changes. Big business will have to change their business model just to remain competitive. The banks, for example, have closed most of their branches. Loads of customers loved going to their local branch, but they were forced to move to banking online. The banks won't remain in a business model where they lose money forever. The way they deal with their workforce will change also. Inside the big corporates, it's a tough time. In many cases, they are heading for tougher times and will be forced to evolve, and nobody inside can stop this change. This is one of the reasons I'm an advocate for people carving out their own path, taking the chance and going into business for themselves. As I've mentioned, there's a risk associated with doing it. But there is a risk of not doing it as well. That's what you have to weigh up. If you want safety, how safe is your role anyway? In a changing marketplace, where is your role going to be in two years, five years, ten years?

"Taking risks and making choices is
what makes life so exciting."

Amy Poehler

CHOICES

After my Dad got over the shock of how much the business had grown in the three months while he was away, he started thinking about me, about my experience, about what I had learned through the process. He sat down with me and asked, "How did it feel?"

"What do you mean?"

He leaned in, asking, "How did it feel having the money pass through your hands?"

What he had known for 30 years, he could see I had learned over the past three months. For the first time in my life, I understood the value of the dollar, because when you're working, and you're getting paid into a bank account, you don't have a true connection with earning money. It goes in and out without you ever touching or seeing it. Because of this, you lose the connection between the labour and the reward.

Now, when you're sweating over a hotplate, mopping floors at 3 am and your body's aching from all the labour, you know why; you have a tangible connection to the money that went through your hands and into the till. Dad had been having that relationship with labour and money for 30 years.

I walked out of the room and stared out at the horizon, and thought to myself, "Holy shit, where have I been? I've been in la-la land. I've had it good."

When he said that to me, that's when the penny dropped. At 35. I wish I learned that when I was 21. I was chasing some dream trying to climb the ranks. I was too busy chasing status to understand what was real and what was important. At the end of the day I wish I had learned that lesson earlier, but the fact is it's never too late to learn the tangible value of money that small business teaches you.

I was 35 when I learned that lesson, I've still got the next 30 years to put that lesson into practice. What an opportunity. I think it was at that moment I truly understood what it was like to run a small business. When you're in corporate, you know about small business in theory, but you're never in the shoes of the person that you are actually selling to.

Most corporate employees talk a big game, but they've never been in the shoes of the small guy out there running a little shop on the street who's trying to put food on the table for his family. I was one of those corporate guys, and then I stepped into my dad's shoes. I now understand the fear that small business owners have because of the uncertainty when they're first starting out.

I had to make that shop work to a certain level to absorb the cost to support my family because I couldn't take it from my dad. He still had to make his own living from the shop. When I was working there, I had to make the shop run on eight cylinders instead of four, as it were. The great thing was that the other four cylinders—the untapped potential—were there, they just weren't firing. My job was to fire them up. I added my own spark, and bang, things took off.

Within three months I tripled revenue, just by connecting the dots. Not because of my dad's inabilities, but because dad didn't have the experience, and he was tired; he didn't want the shop to work harder, but I needed it to. My back was against the wall, I had to make something work. I couldn't get work in Adelaide at the level I was used to working at, and dad had to leave to be with his family in Greece. There was nobody else who could run the shop.

I had no choice.

That's how it seemed, but that's not true. I did have a choice. I could have given up. I could have lowered my standards and took a lesser job back in the banking world. I could have turned completely negative and thrown the towel in. There were plenty of choices I could have taken—but there was only one choice that was a winning choice, and that's the only one I was interested in. I made that choice. I went all in, and I didn't know how I was going to make it work, but I figured it out. Making that choice not only helped my dad out, it helped me discover my greatest passion, it helped me rediscover my spark, and it showed me I didn't need a billion-dollar corporate machine backing me to win in business and life

I think the lesson here is this: when your back is against the wall, sometimes your most creative abilities come out. There is no limit to your imagination when you have no choice – it is here that you reach pure clarity. Some of us place ourselves freely in this scary position. Some end up in this position through circumstance. Some may have exceptional abilities, but lack the courage at that point in time. It's not a lack of desire. Most people just need some help getting started; some need help nurturing their spark. In my current business that's where I can come in and help them because I've been there. I named my company SPARK to remind me every day why I'm doing what I'm doing. I know what it's like to have that fear when you go, "I want to start a business," and then after month four you're going, "Shit, where's the money?" And that fear can extinguish your spark, but it doesn't have to. You can ride the rollercoaster of starting your own business without fear. You might get a scare now and then, that's part of the ride. But you can do it with confidence. You can do it with your spark continuing to grow.

I know about fear. I've been there. But just beyond that fear, when you take that leap of faith anyway, it's there that all the rewards are stored.

When I was out of a job, after I had left the bank and moved back to Adelaide, I thought, "If I don't start earning an income, I'm going to have to start selling some assets." I got through the GFC holding onto all my assets. I got through a global catastrophe, now how am I going to get through this situation? I'm in it because of my circumstance, not because of someone else's or some global circumstance. I've got to get myself out of this situation. When your back is against the wall, you get your most creative. For me, I got clarity through having to take action fast. I remember thinking, "Shit, I'm scared. What am I doing? Dad's going to kill me." I called my mum and told her, "This is what I want to do. This is how I want to do it. What do you think?" She just said, "You know what? Go for it. Do it. The shop needs it." She confessed, "I'm ashamed that the shop is not doing what it used to do." She wanted to see the shop thrive again. She wanted everything to work better. She had lost her spark. That was the message that I needed, just that verbal acknowledgement and backup so that if Dad hit the roof, Mum would be there to calm him down.

At the end of the day, I had to be very cautious about how I operated, because it wasn't my business. That was excellent training for what I do now in my Dealer Group because I support and mentor the planners in the Group, but they own and control 100% of their businesses. I work with them as owners, understanding that it's not mine and yet treat it like it's mine, just like I did with my dad's shop. That's a fascinating skill. The planners within my Dealer Group are small business owners, it's their business. I can't tell them what to do, but I have to influence them in a way to get them to see a certain perspective that they may not be able to see. My job is to cover their blind spots. That's my job, to play defence, be their defence. Their job is to be offence. Go for it. Their job is to be drivers. They've got to drive their business and I'm behind them playing defence for them.

It's like a team. You've got your attackers, and you've got the defenders at the back cleaning up the balls that come through. That's my job. I'm the defence. I'm there to protect. I'm there to cover blind spots. I'm there to communicate, give direction, and help them navigate, but I've got to do it in a way where I'm not telling them what to do because I'm not their boss. They're my clients. My job is to serve them and their best interests to the best of my abilities.

Regardless of what kind of business you start up, you need someone you can seek support and direction from. I'm not saying you should work with me, but I am explaining that small business is hard work. If you try to go it alone, with no support behind you from others, you face an uphill battle. It's hard enough. Be smart and stack as much in your favour as possible.

When planners join my Dealer Group they get all the backend support, but they also get automatic mentorship. I can't recommend highly enough that you ensure you have a great mentor, or several mentors, in your corner to help guide you on your courageous journey to become a business owner, master of your destiny and captain of your fate.

"A spark of passion ignites
the fuel for innovation."
Craig Groeschel

OWNERSHIP

I always thought I would start my own business, but I didn't know when. When is the right time to start a business anyway? The answer is you're never really 100% ready, but you look at the weight of it, you weigh the pros and cons, and you take a leap, or you don't.

I knew that I'll always run a business of my own. Early in my career, I was trying to work out, well, when? What would it be? I never could get to that answer. I just knew in the back of my mind that when the time would come, I would know.

Taking the reigns to run my dad's business was a bit of an emotional rollercoaster. When I started off I thought, "Hey, this might be fun. Something different." But it didn't take long for reality to kick me in the ear and I thought, "Holy shit, I'm running this business. I've gotta make this thing work extra hard because I still need to pay the lifestyle expenses of my mother and father, but I have to increase the revenue to absorb my lifestyle expenses for my family!" That was a kick in the pants, but it got me thinking creatively.

I had no choice but to get all the cylinders firing in that shop, which is why I did what I did. I had to implement the strategies that I mentioned to get those cylinders sparked up, fired up, and ignited to rev the engine harder. Even once we started getting momentum, I realised it wasn't enough. More was required. In small business, you have to keep your foot on the accelerator. I remember thinking, "Oh my God, I've gotta keep this going, not just started, but running non-stop!"

It was a huge learning curve for me, and it was the first step in getting the real world training I needed to start my own business, one that I designed to fit me perfectly.

I've always had this idea around how I could create the perfect job for myself. When I was running the financial planning divisions in the banks, I enjoyed working with financial planners, because what they were trying to do I respected: helping people do well and retire well. After all, I was one myself early in my career as I climbed through the ranks in the bank. It was about helping people.

The reality, however, was a lot of people weren't getting the help they needed, because they just got no advice at all, or, worse still, poor advice, or they were never in a position to make their money work for them. In the end, they had to rely on the pension. I got that, but I also really understood the practice of what giving sound advice was trying to do for the everyday Australian working in a factory or working in a small business. Planners could change the course of the average Australian's financial future, but many Australians just didn't know how to create a better situation. They didn't understand how taxes worked or understanding different investment opportunities they could capitalise on. They just didn't have that kind of knowledge and financial planners did.

So, there was a clear role there, a very purposeful and I think noble role, and I liked that.

I thought to myself, "That's good, that's what I want to be a part of, and if I can help influence those advisors to do the right thing, then my bandwidth of influence is greater because I want to help more and more people." That became my driving purpose.

When my role changed after the merger, the way work was done was also new. All of a sudden I was working with experienced consultants. It was a completely different environment. I was working with people that used to work for Accenture and different people that used to work for EY, PwC etc. It's a different calibre of people. I enjoyed that project-orientated work, but I never liked how a consultant would come in and then leave, and never be accountable for getting the actual job done. It was like the consultants were all saying, "Here's my fee, here's your business plan. See ya." I did like that part of the consultative approach to the strategy and advice they delivered, but I didn't like how consultants just kind of flew in, gave their opinion, got paid and then took off.

I thought to myself, how do I create a situation where I can do consulting, but also deliver for clients? I liked the idea of consulting to a business owner, having that peer-to-peer conversation, or a mentoring conversation, depending on where they are. I wanted to have a real consultative relationship, but also understand their business and understand what they're doing on a day-to-day basis. From my experience, consultants never really understand what happens day-to-day in their client's business. They try to, but they don't. Occasionally they might be industry-specific, and that made sense, but a lot of the consultants weren't industry specific, and each business has its nuances. Unless you spend that time in the business, you never really understand it.

In my mind, a consultant was just skimming the surface and giving a high-level solution and then walking away, and that solution ends up sitting on the cupboard shelf collecting dust for the next 12 months. I thought to myself, "I want to be a consultant, but I don't want to be that kind of consultant. I want to be the consultant that digs in and is there for the long term. They can then point at me and say, 'Mate, you're meant to be helping me here, and you're not.' I want that level of responsibility."

I began thinking about how I could go about creating that kind of job opportunity? I like that consultative relationship. I love the nuances of advice and understand how businesses like that operate. I can comfortably ask, how can I be part of the journey?

Now I'm working in my perfect job, that does just that.

As the owner of a Dealer Group, I can be that consultant with my planners. I want to understand their business, I want to get in there to understand their nuances, and I'm there over the long term because I want to keep them as a client. I don't just come in, deliver a service and off I go.

I've created my perfect job, which is personally satisfying. I look back and think that I'm fortunate to be in a position where I've been able to accumulate all this knowledge and test myself in various roles.

My journey to creating my perfect job and ideal business didn't just happen overnight; it was a process. I got my business competencies and experience in the banks, but my practical training for what I do now I think started when I took over my dad's souvlaki shop. That was the first rubber-hitting-the-road test of running and understanding a small business and implementing a better backend system to power the growth out front. I did it, and it was the first big tick I gave myself as to moving towards creating my ideal business.

After dad got back from Greece and took back the shop, I went out and got a job as general manager at a $4 million turnover advice business, which is a decent-sized business. I started implementing systems and processes I had learned in the Bank and transitioned a whole new company that they'd acquired and integrated it into the business. I met all the objectives that were set up by their Dealer Group and those of the Directors.

I learned a great lesson there about commitment to a strategy. It's one that consultants never really learn because they are not around long enough to do the grunt work of realising a strategy. After working in this business for about a year, the owner came to me and he said, "Arthur, one of your team members had a word with me this morning. He complained that every Monday morning you've run the same meeting, going over the same points, talking about the same strategy." He looked at me to see what I'd say, but neither of us spoke. Then he slowly smiled, and said, "You know what, good on you for being able to do that every week and keeping yourself energised to do it over 12 months. I respect that. The results speak for themselves."

Having that conversation reminded me of a great truth about business. To stick to a strategy, and see it through to completion, can very often feel mundane in the moment. But the mundane creates the magic in the end. I always remember that, and that's what keeps me energised in business. The goal may still be far off, but if we are ever to reach it, we need to bring our best on that day and input the energy required to move us a step closer to achieving our goals. Perhaps things aren't as mundane when the business is yours? I had to find this out for myself but I wasn't quite ready yet.

I believe you've got to wake up on that Monday morning and you've got to have the spark because if you don't have the spark, it channels through. I experienced that first hand in the bank, and I never wanted to experience it again. I nurtured my spark every day. I fanned it into a flame. I know it was the magic maker, and without it I might still have been successful in business, but I'd be miserable in life. I never wanted to goback to that scenario.

I think this is one of the most underrated elements of leadership. If you consider yourself a leader, you've got to take personal responsibility to ensure you have the spark. You have to have that spark inside, and you have to nurture it. Don't ever let it go out.

If I didn't bring that spark each Monday morning, it would set the tone for the rest of the week, and eventually, I would have compromised I would have missed meetings, and before I knew it, the whole team would be off course. That's why I kept my spark front and centre. Those Monday meetings were really about keeping to the program because the last thing you want to do is change things too much. When you make too much changes, you confuse people. At the same time, you've got to battle the monotony that comes with being consistent. You have to bring something fresh to the table every couple of weeks; you have to keep the team engaged as best you can and make it fun. Even with the spark, you lose some people along the way. But I'll tell you this: If you don't have that spark, you'll lose *everyone* along the way!

Working in that company and leading its transformation and growth strategy was just the real-world, non-bank, financial planning practice experience I needed; and regarding results, I knocked it out of the park, so that was good. It was another tickand recognition that I was able to implement my ideas and strategy at that level and that size. The business made the top three in Australia within its Group. Before I started working for them, they were 28th in Australia. 12 months later, we were 3rd. That was a big tick. I thought, "Yep, good, got that one."

I then moved to a $10M+ turnover business, which was similar but the scope was greater because they operated across different platforms. So it was more about, you know, there's the mortgage business, the property advisory business, and the financial planning. So, now I had a multi-disciplined level of business to lead. I was the general manager, but also like a project manager managing all these different things to unite all the various offers and their platforms to consumers. That was a big machine to run and optimise, and another tick for my confidence that I could succeed in the ideal job and business I had in my heart to create.

When I reflect, I see the past five years have been a continual progression towards where I am now. There were different levels, and each one prepared me for the next. Level one, level two, level three, and now I'm at level four, which is my Dealer Group where I support many different businesses with their own identities and their own value propositions, their own geographies and their own vision. This a whole new next level. It's huge in terms of complexity and scale, but for me, it's the perfect challenge and my ideal situation. I know this is where I fire up. I know this is where I'll always have my spark.

I've created my ideal business and perfect role within that business. I'm fortunate in that way because a lot of people at my age aren't doing what they want to do; many don't live their own dream when it comes to business. The reason why is all about risk. To have your own business, to create the business you feel satisfied and fulfilled within, you have to take a risk. It's calculated, it's a good risk, but it's still a risk. Ultimately, you've got to put your wealth on the line. I know I did. In establishing and building SPARK, my Dealer Group, I'm putting my wealth, my personal wealth, on the line to make this work. That's the ultimate step, and that's when you actually can put yourself in that space. You don't have to have my dream or my ideal business situation, but you do have to have your own, and there will be a risk associated with going after it. If you are looking at leaving the corporate world to start your own small business, if you feel the spark fire you up when you think about it I believe you can do it, but it comes at a price. You have to be willing to pay that price. You need courage and faith in yourself to pull it off.

"A candle loses nothing
by lighting another candle."

Italian proverb

SUCCESS

When I took my own big risk and set out to start up and build my own business, the SPARK Advisors Dealer Group, I decided to build it the way I truly wanted it. I didn't want to compromise. I knew the model could work, and it would be a win-win situation for everyone involved, but I had to test it with some real clients. Within a week of deciding to build my business and test my business model, I met Joe. It was perfect timing for both of us.

Joe became one of my pilot planners; one of the initial three that took part in the concept that is now alive and well today. Joe was working for a Group in the capacity of a mortgage broker. He had done financial planning studies and had always had an interest in financial planning and had been an associate financial planner in the past.

He came to me with a business opportunity saying, "Look, as a mortgage broker I see a lot of clients that need financial planning, and I want to refer them to you. On the outcome of that referral, if there's any revenue that you produce, can we come up with a split agreement?"

At the time it was perfect timing in the sense that I was thinking about orchestrating the development of my business offer. I had the opportunity to be selfish and say, "Yeah, yeah, show me all your referrals, and I'll take them on and I'll give you 20% commission, no problem."

As I listened to him, I felt that deep down this guy wanted to become a financial planner, but it just hadn't worked out that way, and he couldn't see how it was still a possibility.

I said to him, "Mate, why give your clients to me? Why not keep them and build yourself a financial planning business?"

He paused at that moment. I had just hit him with the option, the most obvious option, that he hadn't seen or thought he could capture before. I woke him at that point. Joe calls that his eureka moment. He said, "I've just realised that I've got this opportunity sitting under my nose. All I needed was someone unselfish to point it out to me."

I smiled, and said, "Well, mate, take action. Do it. Build yourself an asset, and I'll support you."

He called that his eureka moment where he just realised, "Wow, I can do this myself. I've got the credentials. I've got the desire. It's entrepreneurial. I just have to take action."

My response was to offer my support, "Well, you do it and I'll help you do it; and in helping you do it, I can build my concept at the same time. It's a win for both of us."

Joe took that feedback on and contacted me a short time after and said, "Arthur, how do I make this happen? How do I create this business model?" That's when I made him part of the pilot. I provided him with the initial services of the outsourcing and the administration, licensing, compliance and PI, and so he set up his financial planning company called JZP Financial Planning. From there, all he did was take those mortgage leads and convert them into financial planning outcomes. That was the birth of his financial planning business.

Now, two and a half years later, he's flourishing, he's got 60 clients under advice, and he's making an excellent income. He's doubled his revenue from what he was doing two years ago by unlocking the opportunity that was present around him.

The first few questions I asked him were the questions I ask everyone who is scoping out the possibility of going out on their own.

I ask, "Do you have a business around you today that you haven't realised you do have? Is there an opportunity that's present right under your nose that just with some alternative thinking you could convert into a reality?"

Inevitably, they say to me, "What do you mean by that?"

I say, "Well, if you had no choice but to start a business tomorrow, what would you do first? Who would you speak to first?"

"Well," they say, "friends and family."

"Okay, so would you feel comfortable asking them to work with you in that capacity?"

From there they answer yes or no.

If they say no to that question, I know they're not desperate enough to make it work, and that is OK. The reason is simple: anyone that wants to start a business and has a true belief in what they intend to do and the value they're trying to add to people, why wouldn't they do it with family and friends first? To go into business, you have to back yourself and believe in the value you can offer. If you have that then offering that service to friends and family should be your first client building strategy. They get the value first.

Joe had a lot of family, a lot of friends, and he also had mortgage clients that needed financial planning. So for him, it was a no-brainer. And for me, I would rather see him convert that and build an asset and achieve his goals, rather than me taking it from him and paying myself a bonus. I think Joe saw the opportunity when I said he could start his own business, but also saw in me, someone that wasn't greedy in the sense that I was thinking more about him than myself, and that's why he didn't hesitate to form part of my pilot project.

Damian is another planner who connected with me during the pilot stage of my business model development. Damian already had an established practice. He was working through one of the bank Dealer Groups and just found that what he wanted to do for his clients wasn't in the appetite of his Dealer Group. They were very conservative around the advice, and so he was looking for a more liberal Group that would work with him to deliver the advice that was in his client's best interest, but also within a compliance framework that was supported.

My job as a support is to provide planners with clear, strict guidelines, rules and policies to operate an advice business. We have far more flexibility and being our own AFSL, understand the risk of that model and either accept it or not accept it, whereas the bank aligned channels, are hard line on what they accept or not because their view of risk is a lot more conservative.

The problem with that is it creates a situation where the end advice isn't in the best interest of the client because they're getting the advice they potentially don't want, or the planner loses the client or the opportunity to make them a client because they can't serve them. And so what you've got is a situation where because of the risk to brand, or because they've gone through an enforceable undertaking in the past, the appetite for risk is low, and on their views of ASIC's rules and guidelines, they err on the side of conservatism. But what that does is this: it restricts the amount of advice out there in Australia, and we are under advised in this country because people can't afford it, or the Dealer Groups aren't customer focused enough to deliver advice that consumers want. These Dealer Groups want to dictate exactly what advice is allowable, but in doing so they're getting clients to opt out of seeking advice because no one's willing to help them. When they try to do it themselves, guess what happens? *They either get it right orthey make big mistakes.* Helping consumers avoid these big mistakes is what clearly stands in my mind as the role of a financial planner.

This is the paradigm of the financial advice industry. The major Dealer Groups take a conservative view to protect their own interests. They restrict the amount of advice that could be accessible by people in Australia. That's the quandary we have in this country today: access to advice isn't as abundant as it should be to help everyday Australians.

My view is that you can achieve best interest advice by still being liberal to avoid eliminating the opportunity before it's sought.

Damian found that approach appealing because he wanted to help his clients, but the conservative position of his current Dealer Group wouldn't allow him, and so it contradicted his service model. Therefore he was looking for a new Dealer Group that would work with him rather than against him. That's why he came into the pilot.

Today, Damian is flourishing. His advice process is very neat. We've got exemplary processes in place to understand the risk of the liberal approach to advice through our channel, and we're happy with our system. He's happy because his practice is now growing rather than being restricted.

Now, the third planner in my pilot didn't make it. He's not with our Group today.

Daniel wanted to start his own practice, but he didn't have what it took in the sense that he wasn't willing to put himself out there enough to survive. He only wanted clients that looked a certain way and would pay a certain fee.

Now, when you're starting your own business, my advice to my clients—my clients being the planners—is pound the pavement and pick up every deal you can, no matter what size or shape. Provided you're following all the processes and compliance, take them on and serve them the best you can. It doesn't matter if they're paying you $500 a year or $1500 a year, a client is a client for you right now. Take it. Do it. If it means that you're not going to get the money that you want straight away, that's fine. Work with them, grow them, nurture them, make them feel loved, get referrals from them. A client is still a client. You're growing. When you start a business, that's what's important! You have to grow. You have to have cash flow.

Daniel couldn't get that concept. He wouldn't bend his mandate to accept any clients that didn't want to pay his price. That's why he failed. He starved himself for his own ego or his own unwillingness to accept that he's not going to get the perfect client every time. And you never do, but that person still needs help, and if you're running your own business you need help. Not just them, you need to help yourself.

My point is, don't be restricted. Don't restrict your mind to any opportunity, because a small client could introduce you to a big one if you treat them nicely, show them that you care and show them that you give good advice. So, if in his first 12 monthsa planner says, "I'm only going to accept clients like this," I say, "Mate, if you're going to have that attitude, you're not going to make it. Any client is a client. That client could have a friend or a cousin or a brother or a sister that could be your perfect client. Clients breed clients if you do a good job."

Give yourself the opportunity and work with anyone in the first 12 months that you can help. Have the attitude to help first, worry about the dollars later. When you get your practice to a certain size and you're doing well three or four years down the track you can start segmenting your time. You can start segmenting your client base. You can introduce those clients to someone else, or potentially to a junior that you employ in your practice that can serve them or sell the client.

Your client base represents your business, and your business is yours to sell at the end of the day. Your client in three years time might be someone's client that they want to service today because they're just starting out and they're willing to buy them off you. Someone who is ready to be a true entrepreneur should see that. Someone that's not going to make it lets their point of view take precedence. They're not willing to bend to the realities of starting a business.

I would argue that if they're not willing to fail, that will be the very thing that causes them to fail. That's the lesson with Daniel. He just went back into a salaried job; he didn't make it.

So two of my three original pilots made it. I don't think it's my system and support that they had access to that made them succeed. It helped, but it wasn't the most critical factor of their success. It was the attitude they had going into it which they maintained in the build-up stage of their businesses.

You have to hustle to add value. If you're starting a business and you don't have a pipeline of deals, you must be willing to grab any deal you can. That's the way it is. If you're not going to have that attitude, don't start a business. Don't believe your own bullshit that you think you're too good to serve people who can't afford a premium fee price. I believe planners get into advice because they want to help the everyday person. Yes, we want to have 100 clients that pay us $3,000 a year. Of course we do. Who doesn't? But that takes years to build. You're not going to get it straight off the bat. That could take five years to build. You might have to go through 500 clients to get to the perfect 100. You're not going to get the perfect 100 straight off the bat. You're just not in reality.

Why I started this journey and why I wanted to get into advice in the first place is it empowers you to help people at a higher level. When I started my career, I loved helping people over the counter in the bank as a teller. They came in there and I gave them a good experience. I smiled and gave them money and I processed their transaction and said, "See you later."

It was personal. It was great.

What I learned is that when I was serving these people, I'm looking at their situation and saying, "Oh, did you know you can get a better rate? Did you know that you can earn better interest? You've got a lot of money sitting in your bank account," and this is at the time when the banks started lowering the everyday interest rates to like 0.1%. I thought if this client's got $100,000, why doesn't she put it in a term deposit? So I would ask, "What are you trying to achieve? What's the money for? Are you saving for a house?"

That's why I love financial planning. You can really alter the direction of someone's life by giving them good service and good advice, more than any other job in the bank. That's why I wanted to get into financial planning when I was in the bank and that's why I stayed in it, because it's a deeper relationship, it's a deeper purpose and it's a deeper skill set so that you can alter the course of someone's life for the better.

Running my own Dealer Group now gives me the opportunity to scale my intent by partnering with many independent financial planners who share the same values as I do. It means I can scale my personal intent across many planners. I've designed the system so that I can help more planners give more good advice to help more people in Australia because they bloody need it. We need more advice. So in developing my business, I asked myself, "How can I create a business where I can, within my control and my means, contribute to that purpose?"

I think financial planning is a noble profession, and it's one where you have to care deeply about helping people. At the end of the day, if your purpose as an advisor isn't to genuinely help people reach financial independence, then get out. You shouldn't be in that seat because that's a trusted position. If your intent is not to help, then you shouldn't be in the game;

do something else, because you can damage lives if your intent isn't pure.

So, for myself, I want to work with practices at that business level to equip them, to be able to give good advice, so that my voice is of a different magnitude. It's a much bigger lever. I want to make a significant difference in the lives of others. In my opinion, wanting to make a significant difference is the game every financial planner should be playing.

Ron was another planner who came into SPARK Dealer Group in our start-up stage. He was part of a large wealth channel which was owned by one of the big banks before it was recently sold. 700 advisors in their wealth channel were sold for a billion dollars. That translates to 700 planners going, "Heck, yesterday I was coasting in a secure job, what's going on now? Am I happy with this move? Will I still have a job in six months? What's next?"

That's the nature of financial planning these days. It's no longer the safe play to work in a big bank. Everything is changing in business, and with everything else, the financial planning business model is being disrupted with new models that make more business sense and offer customers a better service and experience.

Ron came to me through a recruitment agent. I had to pay a recruitment fee to get Ron on board, and he was well worth the money. I interviewed him and his friend. Honestly, I thought his friend was going to be the one to choose to work with me so I could support him with his business, but it ended up being Ron.

I'll tell you what, Ron is an absolute terrier. He will go after the deal. He's tenacious. He's someone you want to work with. In his first year, he built himself a six-figure income and he's on track to double that this year. His conviction and attitude are what got him to 100k, but what is taking him to 500k is the system behind his business. That's the value I add. The reason why he's been able to grow is because he's an animal when it comes to taking personal responsibility. He refuses to make excuses. He's got his head in the game, and he's doing the work required to win. But it is also the back end system I provide him that allowed him to not spread himself too thin in the startup stage. He was able to focus on acquiring clients, and we took care of all the admin behind the scenes. The lesson here is no matter what you are doing in business, don't try to do everything. There's too much to do. Find a solution for your backend that best suits your business, so you can focus on pounding the pavement and growing your client base. In Ron's case, he had my team behind him, which allowed him to leverage all his hard business development work to scale fast. Too many people start a business without having a system set up behind them to allow for the business to scale. I say to the planners, "You're paying for us to take care of all the back office stuff. That's going to free up a shit load of time for you. You can choose to sit on the couch, you can choose to sit in the pub, or you can choose to use that time to go hunt down deals. In your first year of business, if you're not pounding the pavement, then you're not serious about making it. You're not willing to put your ego aside in your own best interests; you're not allowing yourself to succeed."

I did it in a kebab shop for my Dad. You can do it for yourself in your own way, too.

Ron, to his credit, used that time wisely. He got onto the BNI chapter in his area; he chose to operate in a market that's growing. He didn't choose his local area out of convenience; rather, he was strategic about the decision. He chose the marketplace he would operate from that was a 30 kilometre drive from where he lives. He was smart because he chose one of those development areas where young families are moving in and there's a lot of mortgages in the area. Fantastic.

He goes, "Right, I can go in that area, I can support those young families with savings plans, super, insurance, money management; the bare essentials." He's nestled himself nicely in that area and he's developing his own brand up there. He's worked his social channels. He's now getting leads from his social media strategy. He put himself out there. He's now the

President of the BNI Group. They elected him within a year to lead the BNI Group, probably because of the quality of character and passion to help others that he's demonstrated in that group. He's a real success story, but I also know he couldn't have done it without the system behind him because every business needs an effective system behind them. However, I don't go out there and tell everyone that because that would defeat the purpose. The system is the invisible superpower to a financial planner's business, but the planner has to always be the visible champion to their clients, the one that connects with clients and advises them with their knowledge and insights. When Ron posts on social media, I say, "Well done, mate. It's your attitude that got you there." And it has. His willingness to take risks, to fail, to get up and keep going, to try again, to take more risks, to win clients one by one is what's made him succeed. Without the right attitude, no support system will help you. But with the right attitude and the right systems and support behind you, there's no limit when it comes to influence and success.

It's not uncommon for planners to have big egos. They want to be in control; they want to control the advice. It's just in their nature, right? I love them, by the way. I think planners, the good ones, are fantastic.

My point is, because of the ego factor a lot of them can't comprehend the concept of being willing to fail to succeed.

Some planners would be great, it would be ideal for them, but they don't realise it. That's how it was with Ron. My conversations in the early days of working with him, he was ringing me for advice all the time. Not in terms of advice to give his clients, he needed advice on the business side of things. He needed guidance on how to run the business and make smart business decisions.

Ron was humble enough to ask for help. It was a game changer for him. Most would try to hide the fact they didn't know how to run their business effectively. Ron bulldozed his ego and got all the help available to him.

I remember the time I was at the Hilton in Brisbane having breakfast. He rung me up and explained, "I'm about to meet this guy, an accountant. He wants to do a Joint Venture. He's going to give me all of his leads."

I put my bagel down and went, "Whoa, whoa, whoa." I said, "How long have you been in business for?"

"Six months."

"And you're ready to wed? You haven't even given yourself a chance. Why do you need him? Why aren't you backing yourself? Why do you need this guy and his leads?"

Ron said he didn't know, it just sounded like a good way to get some quick wins on the board.

I asked, "How long has he been in business for?"

"About 15 years."

"What, so you think you're the first person he's approached? Listen, Ron, you've been doing this for six months, why do you need him?"

"Oh, I need leads, Arthur. All those leads."

I asked him again, "How long have you been in business?"

Again, he says, "Six months."

"Do you think your strategies have had a chance to make it, to mature and deliver fully?"

"No. Not yet."

"So why aren't you backing yourself?"

I let him go and suggested he answer that question before his meeting.

In the end, he went into that meeting and told the guy he wasn't going to joint venture with him.

Literally, a week later another accounting firm approached Ron and said, "Look, we just want to work with you. We like the way you operate and go about your business. You can just work out of our office, and you can service our clients. We don't want to marry. We just want to have a trusted financial planner in our office. Would you be willing to sit alongside us?" Because he said no to the first offer that was not in his best interest anyway, he was able to capitalise on the next one that was.

Because Ron's built such a good reputation, someone in his market said this guy's a good operator, let's work with this guy, but they were greedy because they went straight to marriage, straight to a commitment of a Joint Venture. Whose interest did that guy have in mind? Ron's or his own? And that's something I pointed out to Ron. I said, "Mate, you don't need him. You can do it. I can see what you're doing. I'm backing you. My advice is don't marry too soon. He's going to lock you into an agreement and two years down the line you're going to go, 'Shit, I could have done this on my own, but I've got to give 30% to him now,' and that's going to breed resentment. It's going to end in tears." I gave him good counsel and boosted his confidence because I believed in him, I knew his attitude was solid and he'd get there. I said, "Mate, you don't need to partner with anyone, back yourself. You've got me supporting you. You've got my whole team supporting you. Back yourself. We don't take an equity stake in your business; we just want to support. You own your own business 100%, and in doing so, we get paid. We're not asking for any equity in your business. Don't let others take it. Get out there and keep building."

"Be open to letting yourself evolve."

Gary Vaynerchuck

IGNITE

Every great business started with a spark. Your future business, the one that is just an idea in your mind at the moment, can be great. It can find its expression in the real world around you. It can be a meaningful part of your community. It can and will help many customers.

Do you feel it within you? Can you feel the spark? Is your idea mixed with emotion? If so, nurture that spark. Don't let it fade away. Don't let fear bully you into putting it out. Don't let the perception of safety in the corporate world trick you into giving up on your spark.

The truth is, you've got that spark for a reason. You have it, because you know you want to pursue a career and a business that is more fulfilling and more meaningful. So what is stopping you?

The risk. That's what is in the way. That is the obstacle that you must decide to move beyond, or turn back and settle for what you currently have.

To go out on your own, to start a business, you have to do three things. First, you have to do the numbers. You have to look at what you want to do honestly, do your due diligence, and prove to yourself that it's viable.

Second, you need to feel the spark. It's not good enough to accept the numbers make sense; you need your emotions involved. If you don't feel the spark, that ignition within you when you think of your business idea, it's not the right idea for you. You need the spark. Fear will also be there. Worry and uncertainty will be there. But if the spark is also there, then these other feelings can easily be managed and put in their place.

Third, you have to accept the decision is going to be an emotional one. It's not going to be made purely on the numbers. It's going to be made in your heart and gut. Your head will tow the party line and follow if it has to, but if you put it in charge it will defer a decision. Let your head do the numbers, but trust your heart and gut to decide and leap into starting your own business.

There's risk involved. But it's not just the risk of putting your wealth on the line. It's also the risk of being the only obstacle left in your way to succeed. When you are at the mercy of a boss and a corporation, it's easy when things fail to point the finger, to blame the incompetence of the decision makers, or the lack of funding, or whatever else. When you go out on your own, the only one hindering your success is you. For many, facing that situation is harder than putting their money on the line. But what is on the other side? Not just financial gain, but personal development. Not just meaning in business, but meaning in life.

Becoming a small business owner is a rollercoaster ride. It's not for the faint of heart, but if you are ready to hustle, if you are ready to accept mentorship and guidance, if you're willing to ask for help and put that advice into action, you can make it.

Small business isn't rocket science, but it can launch you to the stars. It can allow you to create a life by design, build a business that is deeply meaningful, and live the dream.

It all starts with a spark.

The magic is in what you do with it.

ABOUT THE AUTHOR

Arthur Kallos is the founder of SPARK ADVISORS. He is passionate about building and growing businesses with a high level of purpose that are dynamic, profitable, and customer-centric. He lives with his wife and three children in Melbourne, Australia.

www.arthurkallos.com

Mick Mooney is a speaker, author and story coach. He helps business leaders capture and express their authentic and insightful stories to entertain, inspire and educate.

www.mickmooney.com

ADDITIONAL INFORMATION ON
SPARK ADVISORS

Spark Advisors is a Boutique Dealer Group founded in 2017 after a successful management buyout of Investors Direct Financial Services, a subsidiary of Investors Direct Financial Group, which was founded in 2001.

We partner with new to market or established financial planning businesses to assist them in growing their client value propositions.

When you join Spark Advisors as an Authorised Representative, you'll benefit from strong systems, compliance support, business mentoring and ongoing professional development. In addition to this is lead generation, a referral partner platform, licensing, implementation & administration, and more - all driven through a tech advice platform.

The Spark system delivers high levels of support for young advisors wanting to start their own financial planning business or more established financial planning practices improve their profitability and client experience.

The Spark System delivers a complete turn-key practice solution to advisors that frees them to spend more time with clients, referral partners and business development prospects while ensuring that effective processes are in place to create and implement advice, ensure high levels of compliance and ultimately shortening sales cycles to increase completed revenue within their reporting period.

Advisors receive a comprehensive support framework and therefore do not have to partner up to overcome what manyadvice businesses are confronted with today such as lack of scale, compliant systems and capacity for new business.

However, those reasons are only the foundation of our vision.

We want to work with you to change the way Australians view financial planning and advice by fundamentally changing the way you engage with your clients.

If you share this passion, we are excited to hear from you.

Call: 0432 132 123

Email: arthurkallos@sparkfg.com.au

Visit: www.sparkfg.com.au